The Young Fathers Art Clinic

Various Artists

Copyright © 2018 Poetic Representations

All rights reserved.

ISBN: 1723039691
ISBN-13: 978-1723039690

Various Artists

THE YOUNG FATHERS ART CLINIC

Various Artists

Various Artists

DEDICATION

To all of the participants of Fathers and Families Center who joined in on the activities, contributed to this book, and inspired others, thank you. Your stories will inspire policymakers to make the systematic changes necessary to lift disenfranchised people out of poverty.

Various Artists

Various Artists

CONTENTS

Introduction   viii

2   Who Am I?   4

3   A Letter To…   34

4   Creative Voices   53

INTRODUCTION

Building a Noble Legacy is a Fathers and Families Center initiative funded by the Robert Wood Johnson Foundation. This is a two-year initiative designed to assist young fathers aged 16-24 to heal from past trauma, grow as parents, providers and partners, and thrive as community leaders. One of the most critical components of Building a Noble Legacy is the art clinic, which helps young fathers of color to find their voices through various forms of art. Every father who comes to us has faced multiple hardships and struggles. Each has joined the program to change their life's trajectory so that they can make a better life for their families.

The art clinic allows fathers the opportunity to give voice to thoughts and feelings in which the fathers may never have shared otherwise. Many saw no point to expressing themselves, but after our time together, they were willing to open up to the possibility that their voices matter. They were able to realize that their voices mattered to others, and not just themselves. They matter to a broader community of which each is a part.

In life, we primarily learn by two methods: experience or example. Many of the participants lacked a positive role model to follow. Due to this, each learned about the society, streets, and the court system often through painful experiences. These painful experiences caused them to reevaluate their past life choices and look for a new direction for their life – landing them at Fathers and Families Center. The art clinic offered each man the opportunity to use their own profound voice and passion to tell their story through original art, written word, or song. Their work serves as an inspiration to those who are willing to listen, whether fellow participant or policymakers.

Few programs like the Art Clinic exist within the communities from which participants come, leaving them with limited opportunities to explore their strengths and vulnerabilities. This book is a collection of stories, testimonies, and activities completed by 20 participants within Building Noble Legacies, which is one of the vehicles used to transition each young man from being victims to heroes in their own story.

Various Artists

*Note: The work was collected anonymously to preserve the privacy of the writers.

Various Artists

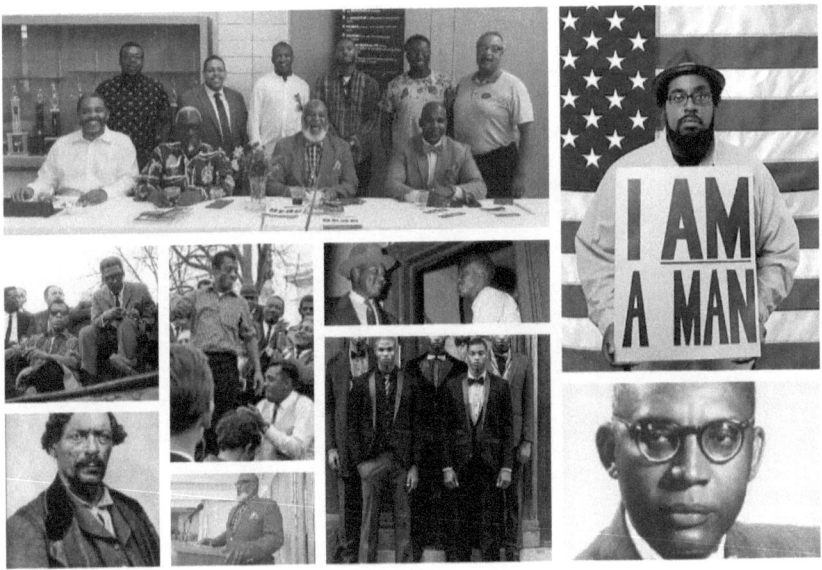

Various Artists

Who Am I?

The following are words written by fathers based on how they view themselves. Each person had a different perspective on who he was at that moment. Some see the good, others see the bad. Some see where they need to go, while others explore how far they have already come in their own journeys.

Who Am I?

I am words forever spoken

A mind that travels without a token

A king on the throne of consciousness

An artist with a constant twist

I am goal driven

The encourager of others

Strength to the weaker

Hope to the lost

Trying to help them be found

Being loud in a world with no sound

– S. Johnson

Art Clinic Teacher

I am EB. A handsome young man. A father of 2 handsome young fellas by the names of K and T. I am a big family person. Friendly, open, kind, non-judgmental. A fan of sports. I am also educated, funny, laid back, and a little soft-hearted.

— Anonymous

I am a man. I am a man with dignity.

I am a father, brother, cousin, uncle, friend, etc.

I am the product of my mom and dad's escapade.

I am a child of God.

I am a good listener, a good friend, and a good person all around.

I am a man who has the same problems as most other people.

I am a man of integrity.

I am honest.

I am loyal.

I am trustworthy.

And most of all, I am me.

- Anonymous

I am a great father.

I am a great man.

I am an Israelite from the Tribe of Judah.

- Anonymous

I am a passionate person, but sometimes it's displaced or misplaced

Sometimes I am hard.

Sometimes I am weak, but I am always fair and mostly meek.

Sometimes, I am indecisive.

Sometimes I am sure, but when I believe in something, my objectives are always pure.

Sometimes, my words are crossed.

Sometimes, my heart gets lost, but sometimes the wires in my brain get crossed and blow a fuse

So I am passionate, fair, firm, weak, insecure, but reassured my actions are stronger than my words.

But when my heart and mind are one, you will see,

I'm honest, caring, loyal, and fun.

                    - Anonymous

I am…

Honest

Cool

Chill

A good person, because I look out for my people

Athletic

Fun

A daddy

Smooth

And more…

- Anonymous

I am me

A lazy person at times, but I am feeling a strive and want to do better than any of my family.

I am a person who wants to strive for success but needs help finding the road.

- Anonymous

I am an Israelite

I am black

I am a prince

I am a lord

I am a father of six

I am a young man getting the skills to become a man

I am God fearing

I am diligent

I am a son of God

I am a brother

I am a righteous man

I am lawful

I am experienced

I am respectful

I am humble

I am confident

I am creative

- Anonymous

Who am I?

I love music!

Music is what I do!

                 -   Anonymous

I am a young, black father

I am a mild-mannered black man

I am a respectful person who cares about others

I am a person who likes to think

I am a person who's always aware

I am a giver to who needs the most

I am smart and am patient when needed

I am an athletic African-American

- Anonymous

I am a father that does not give up.

I am a black male that is strong.

I am a wise man that has a lot of wisdom.

I am a loving person that will share my last.

I am kind.

- Anonymous

I am a young black man in America who has a chip on his shoulders. To other races, I may look like a thug or a criminal of some sort. To me, I am a young father that is trying to mold and prep his daughter for the future. I am a hardworking man who is trying to find his way in society.

- Anonymous

I am me. I am a well-educated indigenous American who has made some mistakes in the past but took these setbacks and applied them to lesson of life. Being born a creature of habit, I finally stood up and vowed to not only change my life for me and my family but to also not allow myself to make excuses like in the past. I will not hold grudges or allow myself to be a victim to redundancy and repetition. My awareness of self-heritage and morality allows me to maintain while having a strong support system that encouraged my ambition and drive. My story will not be one of failure, but one of change, success, and triumph.

- Anonymous

I am a growing adult who is learning to become a basketball player. I am the parent of a four-year-old and am the second oldest to my two little brothers who are 19 and 18. I love life, the animals, and some humans.

- Anonymous

I am an achiever

I am humble

I am observant

I am loyal

I am respectable

I am trustworthy

I am also violent, but aware

I am motivated

I am determined

I am a gentleman

I am active

I am a leader

- Anonymous

Who am I?

A person that is basically trying to change his ways or become a role model to the ones who look up to me.

Who am I?

A person that is really going to overcome the situations I am in and drive for greatness.

Who am I?

A man, not a boy; that has responsibility.

Who am I?

A brother that is from the streets of gang-banging who is going to make a change.

- Anonymous

Who Am I?

I am a man that's been living a terrible life ever since the beginning and I am older, I am looking for a change. I need a change because I been going in and out of prison. I joined the program to become a stronger father and to get some kind of job to support my son.

- A.H.

Who Am I?

I am N. H.

A 19-year-old father

I am the sun and the moon

I am the heat on a hot summer day

I WAS a toxic virus

I WAS a rainy cloud

I WAS a bump on a log

But not anymore

N. H. is a butterfly

N. H. just needed time to grow

                 - N. H.

Who Am I?

R. T. is open, meaning all things that are good; I soak it up. Unfortunately, being open, I soak up the bad as well. R. T. is kind, rough, and gentle at the same time. I'm protective of my love one and understanding to those I fought against, my enemies. R. T. is thoughtful and giving. I care about those who can't protect themselves and the weak. I'm humble, however, easily excitable. R. T. is loyal and committed. R. T. has a sense of purpose in this life and the next.

- R. T.

I am 17 years old, on December 8, 2018.

I have a 4-month-old child.

I am from the southside of Indianapolis.

I want to be a truck driver.

When I was younger, I wanted to be in the streets selling drugs and making fast money.

I was in juvenile a lot of time.

Now I'm close to 18.

I'm getting my mind right by doing what I got to do.

- Anonymous

I am a man that loves my babies and work to take care of them. I am me. I don't know what I am, but I'm working on finding out.

- Anonymous

Who Am I?

A person that is growing spiritually and believes that the human condition is so unstable that without intervention, we will destroy ourselves and torture our children. I want to do more.

- Anonymous

I am a father of a 9 and a 7-year-old girl and a 2-year-old boy. I am raised and born here in Indianapolis. I have been in an out of prison and had very few jobs. This is why I am here; to better myself.

- Anonymous

I am who I say I am. I am a person who was raised in different cities. I have seen a lot of pain and struggles. I also seen a lot of joy and happiness. I've always been a seeker on what in my life. I am an achiever – to be somebody and someone important. I've let pain, anger, and frustration drive me where I wanted to be, but it also had a lot of control over my life. I'm one that seeks peace within myself and life itself.

- W. S.

I am a young black man who aspires to be great. I am driven by having a child that looks up to me. I am motivated by myself because I can do anything, I put my mind to. I am respectful, caring, loving, and intelligent. I have a gift to make people laugh.

- Anonymous

I am an outgoing person. I can be shy sometimes but like to be around other people. I am one to strive for greatness and to always better myself. I am on to help out others and take charge of situations. I am a father of one beautiful little girl who looks up to me.

- Anonymous

I am a father that is trying to be better and stronger.

Also, provide for my family and help others.

I came to Fathers and Families to get more experience to be a father and get experience needed to get a job.

I want to be a better father than my father and be better to my family than my father was to me when I was a child.

- Anonymous

Who am I?

I am me, the shy guy

Till you know me guy

Who am I?

Maybe the guy with the world ambition

But yet don't know what he wants

Who am I?

Maybe that guy who will try, and try again

Just to fail

Who am I?

The guy who was blessed with many chances

Who am I?

Maybe that guy is lost.

             - Anonymous

Various Artists

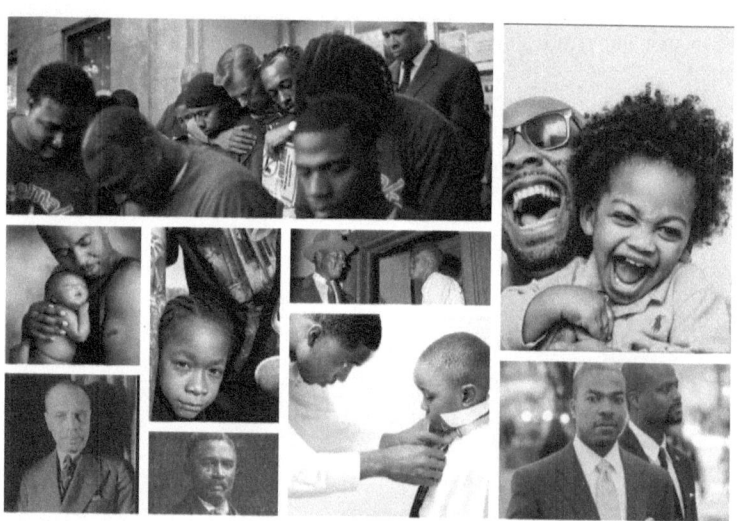

A Letter To…

The following are letters written by participants. These are personal letter written to loved ones, oneself at another age, or people, either in their lives or out of their lives, to whom they had something to say.

A letter to my 10-year-old self

10-year-old self, please listen to your mother and never become like your father. Stay in school, play sports, and protect your family. Never give up and always have faith in yourself and the things you are capable of achieving in life. Remember to become the man that your father was not. Because bad association spoils useful habits. So set goals and finish what you start.

- Anonymous

Dear me at age 10,

    You have such a bright future. You are going to go through things, but you have to stay focused and believe in yourself. You have the tools to be successful and achieve anything in life that your heart desires. You must stay consistent and take good care of yourself. You are a leader and a young king, so act accordingly.

                - Anonymous

Dear Uncle,

 Thanks for motivating me to get out of the streets. Thanks for motivating me to graduate. Thanks for keeping me away from all the bad things I was headed toward. Even though you messed up and started smoking crack, because of all of the things that you showed me, I am still moving forward even if you are not. You have your CDL hazmat endorsement and all, so maybe when I get mine, it will snap you out of it. Then we can be business partners for our family. I kept the family moving forward even when you stopped.

      - Anonymous

To my 10 years old self,

Stop whatever you are doing and do not ever say you want to grow up. Because you grew up too fast and did not prepare to raise a baby and take up adulthood. All because you was NOT ready!

- Anonymous

To myself at 10,

    You are loved. Just because you are not with your biological family, you are loved by the ones that you are with. Do not make any rash decisions based on your feelings. Sometimes our own blood is the ones that hurt us the most. These people love you and care for you. You do not have to run away from that. Life will be easier if you stay.

                      - Anonymous

Dear Mom,

    I know that life was hard for you and you were too young to be a mother when you had me. I do not fault you for your mistakes. I used to hate you for taking me into places and turning me into the person that I was. That is why I gave you drugs. I wanted you to suffer as much as I did. Now, I see that I was wrong. I didn't feel as though I had anyone to turn to but my dudes on the street. They gave me the things I thought I needed. I had money and was able to get all of the things that I wanted. I should have used some of that money to help you get better. I could have stayed around to encourage you to go another way. I am sorry for the things that I have done.

                  - Anonymous

Dear Brother,

    I apologize for not being a good role model for you. I followed dad's footsteps and thought I was doing what I was supposed to do. Now, I look at you and realize that I made a mistake. I don't want you to end up like me, or worse end up like dad. You are special and have a lot of potential. Be the man that you are supposed to be.

                        - Anonymous

A letter to my 10-year-old self.

Dear self,

    You are going to come to crossroads in your life and you are going to make some very bad decisions. You need to think long and hard about every choice you make. Listen to your inner self more and don't ride out with the people you are going to ride out with. Make better friends and hold on to good ones. Tell the others to kick rocks. Above all else, stick to your rules about females. Don't ever break them no matter what. No matter what. Your rules are good and they are there for a reason. Follow them and never bend. Don't break even one. They are important.

                - Anonymous

Dear father,

You are the one who planted a seed in my mother which started the life process for me, but that is all you are. You were not there for my mother. You were not there for any of your kids. You made promises to do stuff for us but never showed up. You disrespected my mother. You beat her up. You even stole from your own mother. What kind of man are you? You were supposed to be my example of what a father should look like. Now that I have children, I pray that I don't end up like you. I want to be nothing like you. You are nothing.

- Anonymous

Dear Self,

Self, I know life seems hard and messy. It seems you can't express to nobody, because of your lack of trust. Man, here's a hug. I love you and I want you to love yourself no matter who may bully you. That doesn't matter. Wake up every morning and tell yourself that you love you, you are a god, and you have a successful future.

- Anonymous

Dear Jr.,

I love you, boy. I love that all you want to do is learn and want dad. I took the step into going back to school to better yours and your brothers and sisters' future. I want you to become something I never was. Dedication and a career are a must.

Daddy loves you all.

- Anonymous

Letter to My Mother

I love you momma for just being a good mom even though we struggled throughout the times. You always made a way even though it was 13 of us and we had to move from house to house. Still, you made a way and all of your kids are strong to this day. Even when daddy would put us out in the rain or snow, you did what you had to do.

I love you, momma.

- Anonymous

Letter to My Love

Baby, I love you. You are the best woman that ever came into my life. You took a lot of bad things out of my life. You brought me closer to God. Thank you so much for being there for me.

- Anonymous

Letter to My Mother,

Mother, I am sorry for not being the man that you wanted me to be. If I had a chance to start life all over again, I could show you how much I cherish you. Mother, I'm sorry about the heartache and pain I brought you. Please forgive me because I'm a better man.

Love you always.

Your son.

- Anonymous

Letter to My Father

I am so glad that after all this time I know you care about me. Dad, I hate the fact we had no productive relationship when I was young. Sometimes I wish things between you and I were different. I always think I could have been so much more. However, after time I feel I needed to go through the things I did to survive in life. Dad, please forgive me for the part I played in our relationship and I forgive you. I'm so happy that we now say we love you to each other.

- Anonymous

Letter to My Father in Heaven

When I turn forty, I hope to be able to look back on my life and not wonder why. The feeling of pain, mercy, and love. Just these very short words a sense of gratefulness kicks in. Thank you. You answered me before I could even finish.

- Anonymous

Dear 10-year-old Self

I should have never come home when we got taken. I felt like my life took the worse turn ever because of it. Hey, I am low-key glad I didn't, because I didn't allow me to have the world's greatest family. It allows me to have the most "baddest" kids and grandkids a person can ask for in my opinion. Because I didn't leave it makes me the proud man, father, brother, son, grandson, son of God, and much more person I am. It makes me strive for more and better for not just myself, family, and friends, but for my enemies as well.

- Anonymous

Various Artists

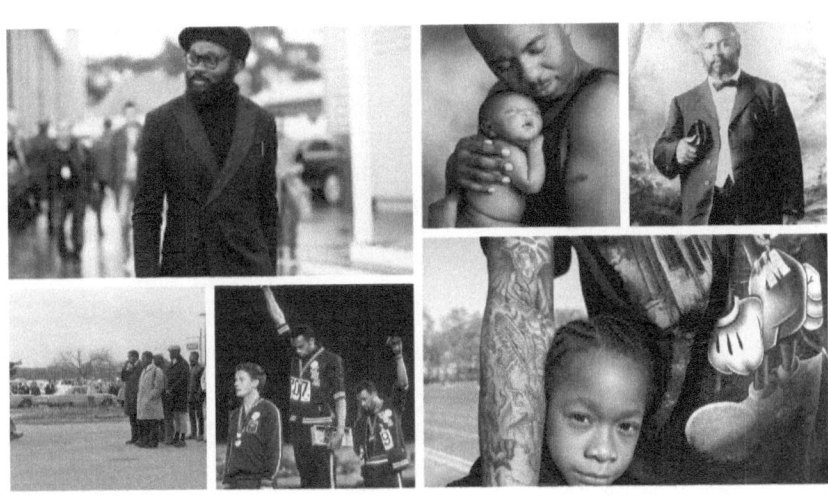

CREATIVE VOICES

In this section, the participants showed their creative talents. Some recreated stories such as "Goldilocks and the Three Bears", "Three Little Pigs", or "Little Red Riding Hood". Some of the stories were not finished during the sessions, but each participant showed a level of creativity that was reflected in the amount written. Others wrote poems. Each participant was allowed to be as creative as desired and insert a little of their world into the art.

In the streets,

When you need peace

The time for violence is never

We need to ridicule it

We need to change the vibes

 To only good ones

I'm anxious to get started

On the movement

I admire the harmony

And the beauty of peace

                 - Anonymous

Once upon a time, there were 3 pigs living in the middle of nowhere. One made a house out of straw. One out of sticks. The last one made a house out of bricks.

Now everyone knew about the wolf and his powerful friends. He would do anything for property. Sort of like the wrong kind of real estate agent. He didn't try to help you, only himself. He would do anything to practically get you to throw your property at him.

One day he pulled up to the street where the three little pigs lived and walked up to the house made of straw. He gave the flimsy door a light tap and told the pig that he was interested in the property.

The pig responded that he was not even selling his place. "You are today", said the wolf. He told the pig that if he did not sell, he will be forced to relocate. Little did the pig know, the wolf called some of his friends to the house already.

A group of wolves arrived on horses. He gave the pig one last chance to move. The pig refused. The wolf gave the go and all the horses surrounded the house and began eating the straw. They ate everything except the furniture. The pig was forced to move.

To be continued…

- Anonymous

We vibe together as we sat under a tree.

The sky is blue

No clouds

We are as peace

Listening to the birds chirp

                       - Anonymous

Three Little Pigs

One day the Big Bad Wolf came from the woods into the hood. He was hungry and searching for food. He came across a straw house that was smelling like food. He decided that he could kick the door down, but was not able. Then he had a better idea. "I can get through the window", the wolf said to himself.

He tried to break the window but was not successful. Then another idea came across the wolf's mind. "Maybe I can kick down the door". So he attempted to kick the door down. Still was not successful.

The another idea, "I can blow the straws down". So he huffed and puffed then blew the straw house down. And the three pigs came out. He had made a fire and had pork chops for dinner.

The end –

- Anonymous

Alien mindset

Cause my thought be outer space

I gotta dream

Like trying to make it to the top

                     - Anonymous

Little Red Riding Hood

Little Red riding in the hood collecting all of the neighborhood worked for. While giving what seems like a good deal, but really Little Red was getting over on the neighborhood. When little Red is done collecting, she began walking back to the house. "Wolf!" A big bad so-called wolf attacked, but Little Red was swift.

While the wolf is starving and fighting for his family, Little Red lives in a mansion on a hill. So the wolf wanted to steal. The same day that Little Red was stealing, but nobody noticed him.

So he ran to the hill and found that there was an older lady out working by the mansion. The wolf crept up and tried to scare the old lady, but she was not afraid. In fact, the old lady began to laugh and break down the wolf's history. The wolf was intrigued and it calmed his heart.

The old lady invited the wolf in for food to stock up on and to get rest before he headed back to town. Little Red got back to the mansion as fast as she could; running with fear of another wolf encounter.

Little Red busted in the house and search for her grandmother, but she had walked down the path for more food resources.

To be continued…

- Anonymous

Beauty rose from the abyss

And my problems became miniscule

Feelings that were residual

Are suddenly invisible

My visions finally vivid

So miss me with all the ridicule

I'm patiently waiting

For tranquility to meet my visual

- Anonymous

Three Little Pigs

Once upon a time, there were Three Little Pigs that had three different houses. A Big Bad Wolf wanted to evict them because they were late on the rent. So the first pig had a house made of wood and the Big Bad Wolf told him that if he didn't have the rent, he would huff and puff till he was evicted. So the wolf huffed and puffed and evicted him.

The second pig had a house made of cheap plastic. Along came the Big Bad Wolf saying, "If you don't have my money today, you are getting evicted". Later that day, the second pig never came up with the money so the Big Bad Wolf huffed and puffed and evicted him.

Now the third pig had a big house made of bricks. Later that day the Big Bad Wolf came by and told the pig, "I need my money today or I will evict you". Later on that day the wolf came back and asked, "do you have my money?" So the third pig paid because it was too cold to be homeless.

- Anonymous

I'm all about the vibe

I like the idea about world peace

You know what world peace looks like

Or could you imagine a world without violence

Yes, I love the vibe

Just talking about world peace

                     - Anonymous

Little Red Riding Hood

Little Red Thot Hood got lost in the hood and couldn't find her way. Until she came to her trap grandma's house and went inside. Then she spotted her grandma and said, "Grandma what big eyes you have". Grandma said, "Girl you know I got cataracts". Then she said, "Grandma what big teeth you have". Grandma said, "What teeth, you know they false."

- Anonymous

Prison is somewhere you don't want to be

Where it smells like butt and feet

Where you better have money on your books

Or they feed you pedigree

Where there is no peace

Trust me brother

Prison is not where you want to be

- Anonymous

Little Red Riding Hood

Once upon a time, there was an evil, lying piece of crap, Little Red Riding Hood. She was walking through the woods with weed cookies for the biker that lived in the woods. When she got to his cabin, she said, "My what bloodshot eyes you have". He replied, "The better to not look at you with". "What a long braid you have". "That's for my crumbs later after I grill you up and eat you". "Look, I brought you cookies". He said, "One, I don't like cookies and two, they are poisoned. Then he jumped up, decapitated her, and threw her on the grill. Later he played soccer with her head.

- Anonymous

Roses are red

Violets are blue

Aliens can be peaceful

So can you

                - Anonymous

Various Artists

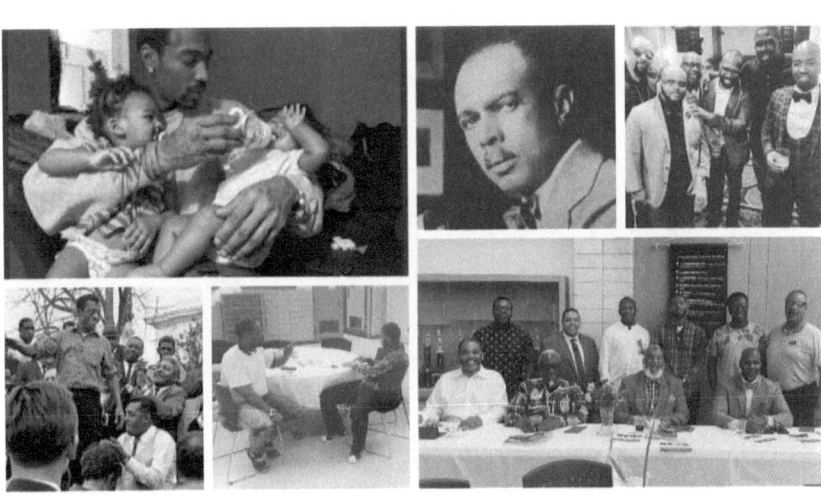

Various Artists

About Fathers and Families Center

Founded in 1993, Fathers and Families Center's mission is to build a noble legacy of fatherhood - assisting fathers in achieving self-sufficiency and in strengthening families to improve the life chances of children.

Our Vision: Each father we serve loves, supports, encourages, and actively participates in his family. Furthermore, each individual and family we serve has a stable and healthy home environment and a productive and fulfilling livelihood.

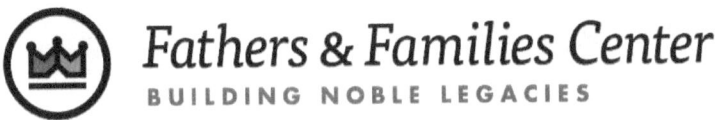

About Forward Promise

Forward Promise is a national program funded by the Robert Wood Johnson Foundation (RWJF) to support culturally-responsive practices that buffer the effects of historical and systemic trauma on boys and young men of color. Forward Promise seeks to build and strengthen the villages that raise and empower boys and young men of color to heal, grow and thrive.

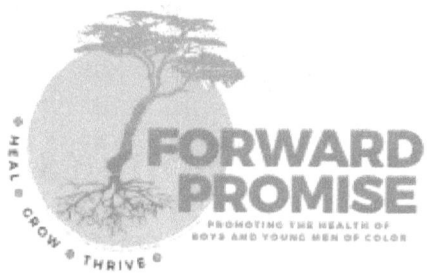

www.ingramcontent.com/pod-product-compliance
Lightning Source LLC
Chambersburg PA
CBHW031536210526
45464CB00003B/1032